T. S. Arthur

The power of kindness and other stories

A book for the example and encouragement of the young

T. S. Arthur

The power of kindness and other stories
A book for the example and encouragement of the young

ISBN/EAN: 9783744748896

Printed in Europe, USA, Canada, Australia, Japan

Cover: Foto ©Suzi / pixelio.de

More available books at **www.hansebooks.com**

THE POWER OF KINDNESS.

And Other Stories.

THE FIRST INTERVIEW

page 21

The Power of Kindness

& Other Stories

T. NELSON & SONS

THE

POWER OF KINDNESS.

And Other Stories.

A BOOK FOR THE EXAMPLE AND ENCOURAGEMENT OF
THE YOUNG.

By T. S. ARTHUR.

———————

LONDON:
T. NELSON AND SONS, PATERNOSTER ROW;
EDINBURGH; AND NEW YORK.

———————

1877.

Contents.

The Power of Kindness.

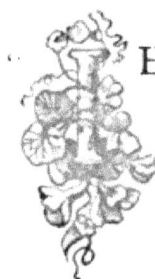

"HATE him!"

Thus, in a loud, angry voice, spoke a lad named Charles Freeman. His face was red, and his fair white brow disfigured by passion.

"Yes, I hate him! and he had better keep his distance from me, or I—"

"What would you do, Charles?" asked the lad's companion, seeing that he paused.

"I don't know what I might not be tempted to do. I would trample upon him as I would upon a snake."

For a boy fourteen years of age, this was a dreadful state of mind to be in. The individual who had offended him was a fellow-student, named William Aiken. The cause of offence we will relate.

Charles Freeman was a self-willed, passionate boy, who hesitated not to break any rule of the institution at which he was receiving his education, provided, in doing so, he felt quite sure of not being found out and punished. On a certain occasion, he, with two or three others, who were planning some act of insubordination, called into the room of William Aiken and asked him to join them.

"It will be such grand sport," said Freeman.

"But will it be right?" asked the more conscientious lad.

"Right or wrong, we are going to do it. Who cares for the president and all the faculty put together? They are a set of hypocrites and oppressors: make the best you can of them."

"They don't ask us to do anything but what is required by the rules of the institution; and then, I think, we ought to obey."

"You are wonderfully inclined to obedience!"

said Charles Freeman, in a sneering voice. "Come, boys! We have mistaken Master Aiken. I did not know before that he was such a milksop. Come!"

The other lads retired with Freeman, but they did not insult Aiken, for they knew him to be kind-hearted and honourable, and felt more disposed to respect him for his objections than to speak harshly to him for entertaining them. Aiken made no reply to the insulting language of the hot-headed, thoughtless Charles Freeman, although his words roused within him an instant feeling of indignation, that almost forced his tongue to utter some strong, retaliating expressions. But he controlled himself, and was very glad, as soon as his visitors had left him, that he had been able to do so.

On the next morning, before daylight, some persons, unknown to the faculty, brought from a neighbouring field a spiteful ram, and tied him, with a strong cord, to a post near the door of the president's dwelling. The president, who was very near-sighted, always read prayers in the chapel at five o'clock in the morning. At the usual hour he descended

from his chamber, and came **out at** his front
door **to** go **to** the chapel, which was distant
some fifty yards. It was a little after break
of day. In the dim morning twilight, the
president could **see** but indistinctly **even** objects
that were very near to him.

The ram, which had, after his fierce struggles
with those **who had** reduced him to a state of
captivity, lain down quietly, roused himself up
at the sound of the opening door, and stood
ready to give the president **a rather warm** re-
ception the moment **he** came within reach of
him.   Unconscious of the danger that menaced
him, the president descended from the door
with **slow** and cautious steps, and received in
his side **a** terrible **blow** from the animal's head,
that threw **him,** some **feet** from where he was
standing, prostrate upon the ground.   For-
tunately the ram had reached within a few
inches of the length **of his** tether when the
blow **was** given, and could **not,** therefore, repeat
it, as the **object** of **his** wrath **was** beyond his
reach.

The president **was** rather severely hurt; so
much so that he was unable to **go to** the chapel

and read morning prayers, and was confined to his chamber for some days. No investigation into the matter was made until after he was able to be about again. Then he assembled all the students together and stated to them what had occurred, and the pain he had endured in consequence, and asked to have the individuals who had been guilty of this outrage designated. All were silent. One student looked at another, and then at the assembled faculty, but no one gave the desired information, although many of those present knew the parties who were engaged in the act. Finding that no one would divulge the names of those who had been guilty of the outrage against him, the president said,—

"Let all who know nothing of this matter rise to their feet."

Charles Freeman was the first to spring up, and one after another followed him, until all had risen except William Aiken. The president paused for some moments, and then ordered the young men to take their seats.

"William Aiken will please to come forward," said the president. As the lad rose from his seat, several of the faculty, who had their eyes upon Freeman, and who had reason for suspecting that he knew about as much of the matter as any one, noticed that he cast a look of anger towards Aiken.

"It seems, then, that you know something about this matter," said the president.

"All I know about it," replied Aiken, "is, that I was applied to by some of my fellow-students to join them in doing what has been done, and that I declined participating in it."

"For what reason, sir?"

"Because I thought it wrong."

"Who were the students that applied to you?"

"I would rather not answer that question, sir."

"But I insist upon it."

"Then I must decline doing so."

"You will be suspended, sir."

"I should regret that," was the lad's manly reply. "But as I have broken no rule of the institution, such a suspension would be no disgrace to me."

The president was perplexed. At this point one of the professors whispered something in his ear, and his eye turned immediately upon Freeman.

"Let Charles Freeman come forward," he said.

With a fluctuating countenance the guilty youth left his seat and approached the faculty.

"Is this one of them?" said the president.

Aiken made no reply.

"Silence is assent," the president remarked; "you can take your seat, young man."

As Aiken moved away, the president, who had rather unjustly fixed upon him the burden of having given information, tacitly, against Freeman, said, addressing the latter :—

"And now, sir, who were your associates in this thing?"

"*I* am no common informer, sir. You had better ask William Aiken. No doubt *he* will tell you," replied the lad.

The president stood thoughtful for a moment, and then said,—

"Gentlemen, you can all retire."

It was as the students were retiring from the room where this proceeding had been conducted that Freeman made the bitter remarks

about Aiken with which our story opens.   It
happened that the subject of them was so close
to him as to hear all he said.   About ten
minutes after this, against the persuasion of a
fellow-student, Freeman went to the room of
Aiken for the satisfaction of telling him, as he
said, "a piece of his mind."   Aiken was sitting
by a table, with his head resting upon his
hand, as Freeman came in.   He looked up,
when his door opened, and, seeing who it was,
rose quickly to his feet, and advanced towards
him a few steps, saying, with a smile, as he
did so :—

"I am glad you have come, Charles.   I had
just made up my mind to go to your room.   Sit
down now, and let us talk this matter over with
as little hard feelings as possible.   I am sure it
need not make us enemies.   If I have been at
any point in the least to blame, I will freely
acknowledge it, and do all in my power to repair any injury that I may have done to you.
Can I do more ?"

"Of course not," replied Charles, completely
subdued by the unexpected manner and words
of Aiken.

"I heard you say, a little while ago, that you hated me," resumed William. "Of course there must be some cause for this feeling. Tell me what it is, Charles."

The kind manner in which Aiken spoke, and the mildness of his voice, completely subdued the lion in the heart of Freeman. He was astonished at himself, and the wonderful revulsion that had taken place, so suddenly, in his feelings.

"I spoke hastily," he said. "But I was blind with anger at being discovered through you."

"But I did not discover you, remember that, Charles."

"If you had risen with the rest——"

"I would not, in word or act, tell a lie, Charles, for my right hand," said Aiken, in an earnest voice, interrupting him. "You must not blame me for this."

"Perhaps I ought not, but——"

Freeman left the sentence unfinished, and rising to his feet, commenced walking the floor of Aiken's room, hurriedly. This was continued for some minutes, when he stopped suddenly, and extending his hand, said,——

"I have thought it all over, William, and I believe I have no cause of complaint against you; but I acknowledge that you have against me. I have insulted you and hated you without a cause. I wish I could act, in all things, from the high principles that govern you."

"Try, Charles, try!" said Aiken with warmth, as he grasped the hand of his fellow-student.

"It will be no use for me to try," returned Freeman, sadly. "I shall be expelled from the institution; my father will be angry; and I shall perhaps be driven, by my hot and hasty spirit, to say something to him that will estrange us, for he is a man of a stern temper."

"Don't fear such consequences," said Aiken kindly. "Leave it to me. I think I can make such representations to the president as will induce him to let the matter drop where it is."

"If you can do so, it may save me from ruin," replied Freeman, with much feeling.

William Aiken was not deceived in his expectations. He represented to the kind-hearted but rather impetuous president the repentant state of Freeman's mind, and the consequences likely to arise if he should be expelled from college. The president made no promises; but nothing more was heard of the subject. From that time the two students were warm friends; and Freeman was not only led to see the beauty and excellence of truth and integrity of character, but to act from the same high principles that governed his noble-minded friend.

There is not one of our young readers who cannot see what sad consequences might have arisen, if William Aiken had not kept down his indignant feelings, and been governed by kindness instead of anger.

Ada and her Pet Fawn.

HERE was once a dear child named
Ada, who was of so sweet a temper
that she only knew how to love; and
the consequence was, that everybody
and everything that could know her,
loved the sweet little girl in return. I do not
believe that a servant in her father's family
ever spoke unkindly to Ada, she was so good.
There are but few of my young readers, I am
afraid, that can say so of themselves. Cook
scolds, the chambermaid is so cross, and nurse
is out of temper, whenever you come near them.
Yes, you know all that; but, my young friends,
I am afraid it is all your own fault. Now,
examine closely your own feelings and conduct,

and see if you do not make this trouble for yourselves. Do you always speak kindly to those around you; and do you always try to give them as little trouble as possible?

As for Ada, everybody loved her; and the reason, as I have already stated, was plain: she didn't know any feeling toward others except that of love. Even the dumb animals would come to her side when she appeared. The cat would rub against her, and purr as she sat in her little chair; and when she went out to play among the flowers, would run after her just as you have seen a favourite dog run after his master. She never passed Lion, the watch-dog, that he didn't wag his great tail, or turn his head to look after her; and if she stopped and spoke to or put her hand upon him, his old limbs would quiver with delight, and his face would actually laugh like a human face. And why was this? It was because love prompted Ada to kind acts towards everything. Love beamed from her innocent countenance, and gave a music to her voice that all ears, even those of dumb animals, were glad to hear. Yes, everything loved Ada, because she was good.

The father of gentle, loving Ada was a rich
English lord—a certain class of wealthy and
distinguished men in England, as most young
readers know, are called lords—and he had a
great estate some miles from London, in which
were many animals; among them, herds of
deer.   When Ada was three or four years old,
her father went to live on this estate.   Around
the fine old mansion into which they removed
were stately trees, green lawns, and beautiful
gardens; and a short distance away, and concealed from view by a thick grove, was the
park where roamed the graceful deer.

Under the shade of those old trees, upon the
smoothly-shaven lawn, or amid the sweet flowers
in the garden, Ada spent many hours every
day, one of the happiest of beings alive.

One morning—it was a few weeks after Ada
had come to live in this fair and beautiful
place—she strayed off a short distance from the
house, being lured away by the bright wild
flowers that grew thickly all around, and with
which she was filling her apron.   At last, when
her tiny apron would not hold a blossom more
without pushing off some other flower, Ada

looked up from the ground, and discovered that
she was out of sight of her house, and among
trees which stood so thickly together that the
sky could scarcely be seen overhead, nor the
light beyond, when she endeavoured to look
between the leafy branches. But Ada did not
feel afraid, for she knew no cause for fear. She
loved everything, and she felt that everything
loved her. There was not any room in her
heart for fear.

Still Ada felt too much alone, and she turned
and sought to find her way out of the woods
and get back again. While yet among the
trees, she heard a noise of feet approaching;
and turning, she saw an animal that was un-
like any she had seen before. It came up close
to her, and neither of them felt afraid. It was
a fawn, only a few months old. The fawn
looked into Ada's face with its dark bright eyes,
and when she spoke to it, and laid her hand
upon its head, the young creature pressed lov-
ingly against the child.

When Ada found her way out of the woods,
and came again upon the green lawn, the young
deer was close by her side. As soon as Lion

saw the fawn, he gave a loud bark, and came
dashing toward the timid creature. But Ada
put her arm around its neck, and said,—

"Don't be afraid. Lion won't hurt you.
Lion is a good dog."

And Lion seemed to understand the act of
Ada, for he stopped short before he reached
them, wagged his tail, and looked curiously at
the new companion which Ada had found.
First he walked round and round, as if the
whole matter was not clear to him. He had
chased deer in his time, and did not seem to
understand why he was not to sink his great
teeth into the tender flank of the gentle creature that had followed his young mistress from
the woods. But he soon appeared to get light
on this difficult subject, for he came up to be
patted by Ada, and did not even growl at
the fawn, nor show any disposition to hurt
it.

The fawn would not stay in the park after
this. Ada's father had it taken back once or
twice, but before the day was gone it managed
to escape, and came to see its newly-found
friend. After this it was permitted to remain;

and every day little Ada fed it with her own hand. When others of the family approached, the timid creature would start away ; but when Ada appeared, it came with confidence to her side.

Ada had a brother two years older than she was. He was different from his sister in not having her innocent mind and loving heart. Sometimes he indulged in a cruel disposition, and often he was ill-tempered. When William saw the fawn he was delighted, and tried to make friends with the gentle animal. But the fawn was afraid of him, and when he tried to come near would run away, or come up to Ada. Then, if William put his hand on it to caress it, the fawn would shrink closer to Ada, and tremble. William did not like it because the fawn would not be friends with him, and wondered why it should be afraid of him, and not of Ada. He did not think that it was because Ada was so good, while he let evil tempers come into his heart.

" But how could the fawn know this ?" ask my young readers. " The fawn couldn't see what was in William's heart."

No; for if it could have done so, it would have been wiser than a human being. But all good affections, let it be remembered, as well as all evil affections, represent themselves in the face, and picture themselves in the eyes; and there is, besides, a sphere of what is good or evil about every one, according to the heart's affections—just as the sphere of a rose is around the flower in its odour, showing its quality. Animals, as well as human beings, can read, by a kind of instinct, the good or evil of any one in his face, and perceive, by a mysterious sense, the sphere of good or evil that surrounds him.

You do not clearly understand this, my young reader; nevertheless it is so. If you are good, others will know it at a glance, and *feel* it when you come near them. And the same will be the case if your hearts are evil.

Ada's pet fawn stayed with her many months, and nothing harmed it. The horns began to push forth, like little knobs, from its head; and afterwards it grew up to be a stately deer, and was sent back to the park. Ada often went to see her favourite, which now had a pair of beautiful branching antlers. It always knew her, and would come up to her side and lick her hand when she held it forth.

Such power has love over even a brute animal.

How to Avoid a Quarrel.

"HERE! lend me your knife, Bill; I've left mine in the house," said Edgar Harris to his younger brother. He spoke in a rude voice, and his manner was imperative.

"No, I won't! Go and get your own knife," replied William, in a tone quite as ungracious as that in which the request, or rather command, had been made.

"I don't wish to go into the house. Give me your knife, I say. I only want it for a minute."

"I never lend my knife, nor give it, either," returned William. "Get your own."

"You are the most disobliging fellow I ever

saw," retorted Edgar angrily, rising up and going into the house to get his own knife. "Don't ever ask me for a favour, for I'll never grant it."

This very unbrotherly conversation took place just beneath the window near which Mr. Harris, the father of the lads, was seated. He overheard it all, and was grieved, as may be supposed, that his sons should treat each other so unkindly. But he said nothing to them then, nor did he let them know that he heard the language that had passed between them.

In a little while Edgar returned, and as he sat down in the place where he had been seated before, he said,—

"No thanks to you for your old knife! Keep it to yourself, and welcome. I wouldn't use it now if you were to give it to me."

"I'm glad you are so independent," retorted William. "I hope you will always be so."

And the boys fretted each other for some time.

On the next day, Edgar was building a house with sticks, and William was rolling a hoop.

By accident the hoop was turned from its right course, and broke down a part of Edgar's house. William was just going to say how sorry he was for the accident, and to offer to repair the damage that was done, when his brother, with his face red with passion, cried out.—

"Just see what you have done! If you don't get away with your hoop, I'll call father. You did it on purpose."

"Do go and call him! I'll go with you," said William, in a sneering, tantalizing tone. "Come, come along now."

For a little while the boys stood and growled at each other like two ill-natured dogs, and then Edgar commenced repairing his house, and William went on rolling his hoop again. The latter was strongly tempted to repeat, in earnest, what he had done at first by accident, by way of retaliation upon his brother for his spiteful manner toward him; but, being naturally of a good disposition, and forgiving in his temper, he soon forgot his bad feelings, and enjoyed his play as much as he had done before.

This little circumstance Mr. Harris had also observed.

A day or two afterwards, Edgar came to his father with a complaint against his brother.

"I never saw such a boy," he said. "He will not do the least thing to oblige me. If I ask him to lend me his knife, or ball, or anything he has, he snaps me up short with a refusal."

"Perhaps you don't ask him right," suggested the father. "Perhaps you don't speak kindly to him. I hardly think that William is ill-disposed and disobliging naturally. There must be some fault on your part, I am sure."

"I don't know how I can be in fault, father," said Edgar.

"William refused to let you have his knife, the other day, although he was not using it himself, did he not?"

"Yes, sir."

"Do you remember how you asked him for it?"

"No, sir, not now, particularly."

"Well, as I happened to overhear you, I can repeat your words, though I hardly think I can get your very tone and manner. Your words were, 'Here, lend me your knife, Bill!' and

your voice and manner **were** exceedingly offensive. I did **not at all** wonder that William refused your request. **If you** had spoken to him
in a kind manner, **I am** sure he would have
handed **you** his knife instantly. **But** no one
likes to be ordered, **in a** domineering way, to do
anything at all. **I** know **you** would resent it
in William, as quickly **as** he resents it **in** you.
Correct **your own** fault, **my** son, **and in a** little
while you **will have no complaint to** make of
William."

Edgar **felt** rebuked. **What his father said**
he saw **to be** true.

"**Whenever you** want **William to do any-**
thing **for you**," continued **the** father, "**use kind**
words instead **of** harsh ones, and **you will find**
him as obliging **as** you could **wish. I** have observed you **both a good deal**, and I notice **that**
you rarely ever speak **to William** in a proper
manner, **but** you are **rude** and overbearing.
Correct **this** evil in yourself, **and all will be**
right with him. Kind **words are far more**
powerful than harsh words, **and their effect a**
hundred-fold greater."

On **the** next **day**, as Edgar **was** at work in

the garden, and William standing at the gate looking on, Edgar wanted a rake that was in the summer-house. He was just going to say, "Go and get me that rake, Bill!" but he checked himself, and made his request in a different form, and in a better tone than those words would have been uttered in.

"Will you get me the small rake that lies in the summer-house, William?" he said. The words and tone involved a request, not a command, and William instantly replied,—

"Certainly;" and bounded away to get the rake for his brother.

"Thank you," said Edgar, as he received the rake.

"Don't you want the watering-pot?" asked William.

"Yes, I do; and you may bring it full of water, if you please," was the reply.

Off William went for the watering-pot, and soon returned with it full of water. As he stood near one of Edgar's flower-beds, he forgot himself, and stepped back with his foot upon a bed of pansies.

" There ! just look at you!" exclaimed Edgar, thrown off his guard.

William, who had felt drawn towards his brother on account of his kind manner, was hurt at this sudden change in his words and tone. He was tempted to retort harshly, and even to set his foot more roughly upon the pansies. But he checked himself, and, turning away, walked slowly from the garden.

Edgar, who had repented of his rude words and unkind manner the moment he had time to think, was very sorry that he had been thrown off his guard, and resolved to be more careful in the future. And he was more careful. The next time he spoke to his brother, it was in a kind and gentle manner, and he saw its effect. Since then, he has been watchful over himself, and now he finds that William is one of the most obliging boys anywhere to be found.

" So much for kind words, my son," said his father, on noticing the great change that had taken place. " Never forget, throughout your whole life, that kind words are far more potent

than harsh ones. I have found them so, and
you have already proved the truth of what I
say."

And so will every one who tries them. Make
the experiment, young friends, and you will find
it to succeed in every case.

The Broken Doll.

———◆———

EARLY all the unhappiness that exists in the world has its origin in the want of a proper control over the desires and passions. This is as true in childhood as in more advanced age. Children are unhappy because they do not possess many things they see; and too often, in endeavouring to obtain what they have no right to, they make themselves still more unhappy. A spirit of covetousness is as bad a spirit as can come into the heart; and whoever has this spirit for a guest, cannot but be, most of his time, very miserable.

Albert Hawkins, I am sorry to say, had given place in his heart to this evil spirit of

covetousness.   Almost everything he saw he
desired to possess.   Had it not been for this,
Albert would have been a very good boy.   He
learned his lessons well, was obedient and at-
tentive at school and at home, and did not
take delight in hurting or annoying dumb animals and insects, as too many boys do.   But
his restless desire to have whatever he saw
marred all this, and produced much unhappiness in his own mind, as well as in the minds
of his parents.

One day, on coming home from school, he
found his sister Ellen playing with a large new
doll that her father had bought for her.

"Oh, isn't it beautiful!" he exclaimed.
"Where did you get it?   Let me have it to
look at."

And Albert caught hold of the doll and almost forced it out of the hands of Ellen, who
resigned it with great reluctance.   He then sat
down and held it in his lap, while Ellen stood
by, half in tears.   She had only had it about
an hour, and she could not bear to let it go
from her.   Albert, in his selfish desire to hold
in his hands the beautiful doll, did not think of

how much pleasure he was depriving his sister, who patiently waited minute after minute to have it restored to her. At last, seeing that her brother still kept possession of the doll, she said, gently and kindly,—

" Won't you give it to me now ?" and she put out her hand to take it as she spoke.

But Albert pushed her hand quickly away, and said,—

" No, no ; I've not done with it yet."

Ellen looked disappointed. But she waited still longer.

" Now, brother, give me my doll, won't you ?" she said.

" Don't be so selfish about your doll," answered Albert, rudely. " You shall have it after a while, when I've done with it."

Ellen now felt so vexed that she could not keep from crying. As soon as Albert saw the tears falling over her face, and heard her sob, he became angry, and throwing the doll upon the floor, exclaimed in a harsh voice,—

" There ! Take your ugly old doll, if you are so selfish about it ! "

As the beautiful figure struck the floor, one

of its delicate hands broke off from the wrist. But even a sight of the injury he had done did not soften the heart of Albert, who left the room feeling very angry towards his sister. He was trying to amuse himself in the yard, about half an hour afterwards, when his mother, who had been out, called to him from the door. He went up to her, and she said,—

. " Albert, how came the hand of Ellen's new doll broken? Do you know? I have asked her about it; but the only answer I can get from her is in tears."

Albert's eyes fell immediately to the ground, while his face became red.

" I hope you did not break it!" the mother said, pained to see this confusion manifested by her boy.

Now Albert, although of a covetous disposition, never told a lie. He was a truthful boy, and that was much in his favour. To lie is most wicked and despicable. There is no meaner character than a liar.

" Yes, ma'am, I broke it," he replied, without any equivocation.

" How did you do that, Albert ? " asked his mother.

" Ellen would not let me hold it, and I got angry and threw it upon the floor. I didn't mean to break it."

At this confession, Albert's mother was very much grieved.

"But what right had you to Ellen's doll ? " she asked.

" I wanted to hold it."

" But it was your sister's, not yours ; and if she did not wish you to have it, that was no reason why you should get angry and break it."

" But, indeed, mother, I didn't mean to break it."

" I don't suppose you did. I should be very sorry to think you were so wicked. Still, you have been guilty of a great wrong to your sister ; and to this you have no doubt been led by indulging in that covetous spirit of which I have so often talked to you, and which, if not overcome, may lead you into some great evil when you become a man. But tell me just how it happened."

And Albert truthfully related what had passed.

"I cannot tell you how much all this grieves me," his mother said. "Ellen never interferes with your pleasures, and never covets your playthings nor books, but you give her no peace with anything she has. If your father brings each of you home a book, yours is thrown aside in a few moments, and you want to look at hers. It is this covetous spirit— this desiring to have what belongs to another —that leads to stealing; and unless you put it away from your heart, you will be in great danger of more temptations than now assail you. Poor Ellen! Her heart is almost broken about her doll."

"I am very sorry, mother," replied Albert in a penitent voice. "I wish I hadn't touched her doll. Don't you think it can be mended? Can't I buy her a new hand for it? I will take the money out of my box."

"We will see about that, my dear. If you can restore the hand, I think it is your duty to do so. It will be nothing but simple justice, and we should all be just one towards another

in little as well as in great things. But your
first duty is to go to Ellen and try to comfort
her in her affliction, for it is a great grief for
her to have her beautiful doll broken. I found
her just now crying bitterly."

All Albert's better feelings came back into
his heart. He felt very sorry for Ellen, and
went in immediately to the room where she
was. He found her with her head leaning
down upon a table, weeping.

"Sister Ellen!" he said, speaking earnestly,
"I am so sorry I broke your doll's hand.
Don't cry, and I will take money out of my
box, and buy you a new hand for it."

Albert's voice was so kind, and so full of
sympathy, that Ellen felt better in a moment.
She lifted her head from the table and looked
round into her brother's face.

"You will forgive me, won't you, sister?"
he said. "I was angry and wicked, but I am
very sorry, and will try and never trouble you
any more. After dinner we will go out, and
see if we can't find another hand, and I will
buy it for you out of my own money."

Ellen's tears all dried up; and she said in a

kind, gentle way, that she forgave her brother. After dinner they went out together, and Albert found a new hand, and bought it for his sister. The doll is now as good as it was before; and what is better, Albert has learned to restrain his covetous spirit, and to leave Ellen happy in the enjoyment of what is her own.

Harsh Words and Kind Words.

WILLIAM BAKER, and his brother Thomas, and sister Ellen, were playing on the green lawn in front of their mother's door, when a lad named Henry Green came along the road, and seeing the children enjoying themselves, opened the gate and came in. He was rather an ill-natured boy, and generally took more pleasure in teasing and annoying others than in being happy with them. When William saw him coming in through the gate, he called to him and said, in a harsh way,—

"You may just keep oat, Henry Green, and go about your business! We don't want you here."

But Henry did not in the least regard what William said. He came directly forward, and joined in the sport as freely as if he had been invited instead of repulsed. In a little while he began to pull Ellen about rudely, and to push Thomas so as nearly to throw them down upon the grass.

"Go home, Henry Green! Nobody sent for you! Nobody wants you here!" said William Baker, in an angry tone.

It was of no use, however. William might as well have spoken to the wind. His words were unheeded by Henry, whose conduct became ruder and more offensive.

Mrs. Baker, who sat at the window, saw and heard all that was passing. As soon as she could catch the eye of her excited son, she beckoned him to come to her, which he promptly did.

"Try kind words on him," she said; "you will find them more powerful than harsh words. You spoke very harshly to Henry when he came in, and I was sorry to hear it."

"It won't do any good, mother. He's a rude,

bad boy, and I wish he would stay at home. Won't you make him go home?"

"First go and speak to him in a gentler way than you did just now. Try to subdue him with kindness."

William felt that he had been wrong in letting his angry feelings express themselves in angry words. So he left his mother and went down upon the lawn, where Henry was amusing himself by trying to trip up the children with a long stick, as they ran about on the green.

"Henry," he said, cheerfully and pleasantly, "if you were fishing in the river; and I were to come and throw stones in where your line fell, and scare away all the fish, would you like it?"

"No, I should not," replied the lad.

"It wouldn't be kind in me?"

"No, of course it wouldn't."

"Well, now, Henry"—William tried to smile and to speak very pleasantly—"we are playing here and trying to enjoy ourselves. Is it right for you to come and interrupt us by tripping up our feet, pulling us about, and pushing us down? I am sure you will not think so if you reflect a moment. So don't do it any more, Henry."

"No, I will not," replied Henry promptly. "I am sorry that I disturbed you. I didn't think what I was doing. And now I remember, father told me not to stay, and I must run home."

So Henry Green went quickly away, and the children were left to enjoy themselves.

"Didn't I tell you that kind words were more powerful than harsh words, William?" said his mother, after Henry had gone away. "When we speak harshly to our fellows, we arouse their angry feelings, and then evil spirits have power over them; but when we speak kindly, we affect them with gentleness, and good spirits flow into this latter state, and excite in them better thoughts and intentions. How quickly Henry changed, when you changed your manner and the character of your language. Do not forget this, my son. Do not forget that kind words have double the power of harsh ones."

A Noble Act.

"WHAT have you there, boys?" asked Captain Bland.

"A ship," replied one of the lads who were passing the captain's neat cottage.

"A ship! Let me see;" and the captain took the little vessel, and examined it with as much fondness as a child does a pretty toy. "Very fair indeed; who made it?"

"I did," replied one of the boys.

"You, indeed! Do you mean to be a sailor, Harry?"

"I don't know. I want father to get me into the navy."

"As a midshipman?"

" Yes, sir."

Captain Bland shook his head.

"Better be a farmer, a physician, or a merchant."

"Why so, captain ? " asked Harry.

" All these are engaged in the doing of things directly useful to society."

"But I am sure, captain, that those who defend us against our enemies, and protect all who are engaged in commerce from wicked pirates, are doing what is useful to society."

"Their use, my lad," replied Captain Bland, "is certainly a most important one ; but we may call it rather negative than positive. The civilian is engaged in building up and sustaining society in doing good, through his active employment, to his fellow-men. But military and naval officers do not produce anything ; they only protect and defend."

"But if they did not protect and defend, captain, evil men would destroy society. It would be of no use for the civilian to endeavour to build up, if there were none to fight against the enemies of the state."

"Very true, my lad. The brave defender of

his country cannot be dispensed with, and we give him all honour. Still, the use of defence and protection is not so high as the use of building up and sustaining. The thorn that wounds the hand stretched forth to pluck the flower is not so much esteemed, nor of so much worth, as the blossom it was meant to guard. Still, the thorn performs a great use. Precisely a similar use does the soldier or naval officer perform to society; and it will be for you, my lad, to decide as to which position you would rather fill."

"I never thought of that, captain," said one of the lads. "But I can see clearly how it is. And yet I think those men who risk their lives for us in war, deserve great honour. They leave their homes, and remain away, sometimes for years, deprived of all the comforts and blessings that civilians enjoy, suffering frequently great hardships, and risking their lives to defend their country from her enemies."

"It is all as you say," replied Captain Bland; "and they do, indeed, deserve great honour. Their calling is one that exposes them to imminent peril, and requires them to make many sacrifices; and they encounter not this peril and sacrifice for their own good, but for the good of others. Their lives do not pass so evenly as do the lives of men who spend their days in the peaceful pursuits of business, art, or literature; and we could hardly wonder if they lost some of the gentler attributes of the human heart. In some cases this is so; but, in very many cases, the reverse is true. We find the man who goes fearlessly into battle, and there, in defence of his country, deals death and destruction unsparingly upon her enemies, acting, when occasion offers, from the most humane sentiments, and jeopardizing his life to save the life of a single individual. Let me relate to you a true story in illustration of what I say.

"When the unhappy war that was waged by the American troops in Mexico broke out, a lieutenant in the navy, who had a quiet berth at Washington, felt it to be his duty to go to the scene of strife, and therefore asked to be ordered to the Gulf of Mexico. His request was complied with, and he received orders to

go on board the steamer *Mississippi*, Commodore
Perry, then about to sail from Norfolk to Vera
Cruz.

"Soon after the *Mississippi* arrived out, and
before the city and castle were taken, a terrible
'norther' sprung up, and destroyed much ship-
ping in the harbour. One vessel, on which
were a number of passengers, was thrown high
upon a reef; and when morning broke, the
heavy sea was making a clear breach through
her. She lay about a mile from the *Mississippi*, and it soon became known on board the
steamer that a mother and her infant were
in the wreck, and that, unless succour came
speedily, they would perish. The lieutenant
of whom I speak immediately ordered out a
boat's crew, and although the sea was rolling tremendously, and the 'norther' still blow-
ing a hurricane, started to the rescue. Right
in the teeth of the wind were the men com-
pelled to pull their boat, and so slowly did they
proceed that it took more than two hours to
gain the wreck.

"At one time they actually gave up, and the
oars lay inactive in their hands. At this crisis,

the brave but humane officer, pointing with one hand to the fortress of San Juan de Ulloa, upon which a fire had already commenced, and with the other to the wreck, exclaimed, with noble enthusiasm,—

"'Pull away, men! I would rather save the life of that woman and her child, than have the honour of taking the castle!'

"Struck by the noble, unselfish, and truly humane feelings of their officer, the crew bent with new vigour to their oars. In a little while the wreck was gained, and the brave lieutenant had the pleasure of receiving into his arms the almost inanimate form of the woman, who had been lashed to the deck, and over whom the waves had been beating, at intervals, all night.

"In writing home to his friends, after the excitement of the adventure was over, the officer spoke of the moment when he rescued that mother and child from the wreck as the proudest of his life.

"Afterwards he took part in the bombard-ment of Vera Cruz, and had command, in turn, of the naval battery, where he faithfully and

energetically performed his duty as an officer
in the service of his country.   He was among
the first of those who entered the captured city;
but pain, not pleasure, filled his mind, as he
looked around and saw death and destruction on
every hand.   The arms of his country had been
successful ; the officer had bravely contributed
his part in the work ; but he frankly owns
that he experienced far more delight in saving
the woman he had borne from the wreck, than
he could have felt had he been the commander
of the army that reduced the city.

"Wherever duty calls, my lads," concluded
the captain, "you will find that brave officer.
He will never shrink from the post of danger,
if his country have need of him, nor will he
ever be deaf to the appeal of humanity ; but so
long as he is a true man, just so long will he
delight more in saving than in destroying."

Emma Lee and her Sixpence.

EMMA'S aunt had given her a sixpence, and now the question was, what should she buy with it?

"I'll tell you what I will do, mother," she said, changing her mind for the tenth time.

"Well, dear, what have you determined upon now?"

"I'll save my sixpence until I get a good many more, and then I'll buy me a handsome wax doll. Wouldn't you do that, mother, if you were me?"

"If I were you, I suppose I should do just as you will," replied Emma's mother, smiling.

"But, mother, don't you think that would

be a nice way to do? I get a good many pennies and sixpences, you know, and could soon save enough to buy me a beautiful wax doll."

"I think it would be better," said Mrs. Lee, "for you to save up your money and buy something worth having."

"Isn't a large wax doll worth having?"

"Oh yes; for a little girl like you."

"Then I'll save up my money, until I get enough to buy me a doll as big as Sarah Johnson's."

In about an hour afterwards, Emma came to her mother, and said,—

"I've just thought what I will do with my sixpence. I saw such a beautiful book at a shop yesterday! It was full of pictures, and the price was just sixpence. I'll buy that book."

"But didn't you say, a little while ago, that you were going to save your money until you had enough to buy a doll?"

"I know I did, mother; but I didn't think about the book then. And it will take so long before I can save up money enough to get a new doll. I think I will buy the book."

" Very well, dear," replied Mrs. Lee.

Not long after, Emma changed her mind again.

On the next day her mother said to her,—

" Your aunt Mary is very ill, and I am going to see her.　Do you wish to go with me ?"

" Yes, mother, I should like to go.　I am so sorry that aunt Mary is ill.　What ails her ?"

" She is never very well, and the least cold makes her worse.　The last time she was here she took cold."

As they were about leaving the house, Emma said,—

" I'll take my sixpence with me, and spend it, mother."

" What are you going to buy ?" asked Mrs. Lee.

" I don't know," replied Emma.　" Sometimes I think I will buy some cakes ; and then I think I will get a whole sixpence worth of cream candy—I like it so."

" Have you forgotten the book ?"

" Oh no.　Sometimes I think I will buy the book.　Indeed, I don't know what to buy."

In this undecided state of mind, Emma

started with her mother to see her aunt. They
had not gone far before they met a poor woman
with some very pretty bunches of flowers for
sale. She carried them on a tray. She stopped
before Mrs. Lee and her little girl, and asked if
they would not buy some flowers.

"How much are they a bunch?" asked
Emma.

"Sixpence," replied the woman.

"Mother, I'll tell you what I will do with
my sixpence," said Emma, her face brightening
with the thought that came into her mind. "I
will buy a bunch of flowers for aunt Mary.
You know how she loves flowers. Can't I do
it, mother?"

"Oh yes, dear. Do it, by all means, if you
think you can give up the nice cream candy or
the picture book for the sake of gratifying your
aunt."

Emma did not hesitate a moment, but selected
a very handsome bunch of flowers, and paid her
sixpence to the woman with a feeling of real
pleasure.

Aunt Mary was very much pleased with the
bouquet Emma brought her.

" The sight of these flowers, and their delightful perfume, really makes me feel better," she said, after she had held them in her hand for a little while. " I am very much obliged to my niece for thinking of me."

That evening Emma looked up from a book which her mother had bought her as they returned home from aunt Mary's, and with which she had been much entertained, and said,—

" I think the spending of my sixpence gave me a double pleasure."

" How so, dear ?" asked Mrs. Lee.

" I made aunt happy, and the flower-woman too. Didn't you notice how pleased the flower woman looked ? I shouldn't wonder if she had little children at home, and thought about the bread that sixpence would buy them when I paid it to her. Don't you think she did ?"

" I cannot tell that, Emma," replied her mother ; " but I shouldn't at all wonder if it were as you suppose. And so it gives you pleasure to think you have made others happy ?"

" Indeed it does."

" Acts of kindness," replied Emma's mother, " always produce a feeling of pleasure. This

every one may know.   And it is the purest and
truest pleasure we experience in this world.
Try and remember this little incident of the
flowers as long as you live, my child ; and let
the thought of it remind you that every act of
self-denial brings to the one who makes it a
sweet delight."

The Timely Aid.

"TAKE care of that wolf, my son," said Mrs. Maylie to a boy about twelve years old, who had come from school in a very ill humour with a playmate, and kept saying harsh things about him, which were but oral evidences of the unkind feelings he cherished within.

"What wolf, mother?" asked Alfred, looking up with surprise.

"The wolf in your heart. Have you already forgotten what I told you last evening about the wild beasts within you?"

"But you told us too," spoke up little Emily, "about the innocent lambs. There are gentle and good animals in us, as well as fierce and evil ones."

"Oh yes. Good affections are the innocent animals of your hearts, and evil affections the cruel beasts of prey that are lurking there, ever ready, if you will permit them, to rise up and destroy your good affections. Take care, my children, how you permit the wild beasts to rage. In a moment that you know not, they may ravage some sweet spot."

"But what did you mean by saying that there was a *wolf* in brother Alfred? Tell us the meaning of that, mother."

"Yes, do, mother," joined in Alfred, whose ill humour had already begun to subside. "I want to know what the wolf in my heart means."

"Do you know anything about the nature of wolves?" asked Mrs. Maylie.

"They are very cruel, and love to seize and eat up dear little innocent lambs," said Emily.

"Yes, my children, their nature is cruel, and they prey upon innocent creatures. Until now, Alfred, you have always loved to be with your playmate, William Jarvis."

Alfred was silent.

" Was it not so, my dear ?"

" Yes, ma'am ; I used to like him."

" Frequently you would get from me a fine large apple, or a choice flower from the garden, to present to him. But the tender and innocent feelings that prompted you to do this have perished. Some wolf has rushed in and destroyed them. Is it not so ?"

Alfred sat in thoughtful silence.

" Think, my son," continued Mrs. Maylie, " how innocent, like gentle lambs, were your feelings until now. When you thought of William, it was with kindness. When you played by his side, it was with a warm, even tender regard. But it is not so now. Some beast of prey has devoured these lambs—these innocent creatures that sported in your bosom. If the angry, raging wolf has not eaten them up, where are they ? Before you permitted yourself to feel anger against William, gentle creatures leaped about happily in your breast ; but you feel them no longer—only the wolf is there. Will you let him still rage, and devour your lambs, or will you drive him out ?"

" I will drive him out, mother, if I can. How shall I do it ?" Alfred said earnestly, and with a troubled look.

" By resisting him even unto the death. You have the power. You have weapons that will prevail. Try to forget the fault of William ; try to excuse him ; think of his good qualities; and assure yourself of what I know to be true —that he never meant to offend you. If the angry wolf growl in your bosom, thrust bravely at him, as you would, were you, weapon in hand, defending a sheepfold ; and he will and must retire, or die at your feet. Then innocent lambs will again be seen, and their sports delight your heart. Then you will feel no more anger towards your young friend, but love instead."

" I don't think I am angry with William, mother," Alfred said.

" But you were just now."

" Yes ; but the wolf is no longer in my heart," the boy replied smiling. " He has been driven out."

" And innocent creatures can now sport there unharmed. I am glad of it. Do not again,

Alfred, do not any of you, my children, permit ravenous beasts to prey upon the lambs of your flocks. Fly from them in as much terror as you would fly from the presence of a wolf, a tiger, or a lion, were one to meet you in a forest. They are equally hurtful—one injures the body, the other the soul."

"Tell us now, mother, about the wolf that had nearly killed uncle Harper when he was a little boy no bigger than me," spoke up Charley, the youngest of Mrs. Maylie's treasures.

"Oh yes, mother, tell us all about it," said Alfred.

"I've told you that very often," the mother returned.

"But we want to hear it again. Tell it to us; won't you, mother?"

"Oh, certainly. Many years ago, when I was a little girl not bigger than Emily, we lived at the foot of a high mountain, in a wild, unsettled country. There were but few neighbours, and they were at great distances from us. At that time bears, wolves, and panthers were in the region where we lived, and often destroyed the sheep of the settlers, and otherwise annoyed them. The men used frequently to go out and hunt them, and kill off these their forest enemies in great numbers.

" One day, when your uncle Harper was about five years old, our father took us in his waggon to visit a neighbour about six miles up among the mountains. This neighbour had a little boy just Harper's age, and they were together in the garden and about the house all the morning. After dinner, they were dressed up nicely, and again went out to play.

" ' Come,' said Harper's companion, ' let us go and see brother Allen's bird-trap. He caught three pheasants yesterday. Maybe we'll find one in it to-day.'

" Harper was very willing to go. And so they started right into the woods; for the forest came up close to the house, and went off quite out of sight. They had not been gone long before a neighbour, who lived about a mile off, came over to say that a very large wolf had been seen a few hours before.

" ' Where is Harper?' my mother asked quickly, going to the door and looking out.

" ' I saw him a little while ago, playing about here with Johnny,' some one replied.

" ' But where is he now?' and our mother went out of doors, looking all around the house and in the garden.

" ' They've gone off to my bird-trap, without doubt,' said Allen, a stout boy about sixteen years of age. ' Johnny has been there several times within a day or two.'

" ' Do run and see,' urged our mother. Allen took up his gun and started off quickly towards the place where he had set his bird-trap. Two or three took other directions; for, now that it was known a wolf had been seen, all were alarmed at the absence of the children. In about five minutes after Allen had left the house, we were startled by the sharp crack of a rifle in the direction he had taken. For the next five minutes we waited in dreadful suspense; then we were gladdened by the sight of Allen, bringing home the two children. But when we heard all that had occurred, we trembled from head to foot. Allen had gone quickly towards the place where he expected to find the little truants. When he came in sight of the trap, he saw them on the ground close to it, and was just going to call out to them to take care or they would spring it, when the dark body of a large wolf came quickly in between him and the children. There was not a moment to be lost; if the cruel beast reached them, destruction would be inevitable. Quickly presenting his rifle, he took a steady aim and fired. A fierce howl answered the report: as the smoke arose from before his eyes, he saw the 'gaunt gray robber' of the wilderness rolling upon the ground. The bullet had sped with unerring certainty.

"How thankful we were," added Mrs. Maylie, "when, knowing how great had been the danger, we saw the children safe from all harm!"

"Does uncle Harper remember it?" asked Charley.

"Yes; he says he can just remember something about it; but he was a very little boy then."

"That was a *real* wolf," remarked Emily;

" but the wolves, and tigers, and lambs you have been telling us about are not real, are they? Real animals can't live in us."

" If there was nothing real about them, could they hurt you, dear?"

" No."

" But the wolves I spoke about do hurt you. Must they not be real then?"

" Not real like the big hairy wolf I saw at the show?"

" Oh no; not real like that; not clothed in flesh; but still real, so far as power to harm you is concerned: and surely that is reality enough. Don't you think so?"

" Yes, real that way. But still," Alfred said, " I can't understand how a real wolf can be in me; for a wolf is much bigger than I am."

" But I don't mean a flesh and blood wolf, but something in you that partakes of the wolf's cruel nature, and, like the wolf, seeks to destroy all in you that is good, and harmless, and innocent. There may be in you something that corresponds to the fierce nature of the wolf, and something that corresponds to the gentle nature of the lamb. Both of these cannot be active at the same time. If you let the wolf rule, your gentle lambs, as I before told you, will be destroyed."

The children now understood their mother better, though they could not clearly comprehend all that was meant by the wild beasts and innocent creatures of the human heart.

The Double Fault.

"WHY, Arthur," exclaimed Mrs. Mason, on coming into the room where she had left her two boys playing, and finding one of them there with a bunch of flowers in his hand; "how came you to pull my flowers? Haven't I positively forbidden you to do so?"

"I did not do it, mother. I did not do it. It was John."

"Where is John?"

"He's in the yard."

"Call him in," said Mrs. Mason.

While Arthur was at the window calling to his brother, Mr. Mason, the father, came into the room.

"John has been pulling my flowers. Isn't it too bad that a boy as big as he is should have so little consideration? They were coming out into bloom beautifully."

Just then John entered, with a bunch of flowers also in his hand.

"John, how came you to pull my flowers?" said Mrs. Mason. "You knew it was wrong."

"I did not think, when I pulled off a rosebud and two or three larkspurs," replied John.

"Two or three larkspurs and a rosebud! Why, your hand is full of flowers."

"Oh, but William Jones gave me all but the larkspurs and the rosebud. Indeed, mother, I didn't touch any more; and I am sorry I took them; but I forgot that it was wrong when I did so."

"But Arthur says you pulled that large bunch in his hand."

"Arthur knows I didn't. He knows he pulled them himself, and that I told him he'd better not do it; but he said he'd as much right to the flowers as I had."

Mr. and Mrs. Mason both looked at Arthur in surprise and displeasure. His countenance showed that he had been guilty of wrongly accusing his brother.

"Is it true that you did pull the flowers, Arthur?" asked his mother.

But Arthur was silent.

"Speak, sir!" said the father sternly. "Did you pull the flowers?"

"Yes, sir."

"And then falsely accused your brother of the wrong you had done. That my boy should be guilty of an evil act like this! I could not have believed it. It is a wicked thing to tell a lie to hide a fault, simply; but falsely to accuse another of what we have ourselves done, is still more wicked. Can it be possible that a son of mine has fallen so low? It grieves me to the heart."

Mr. Mason spoke as he felt. He was deeply grieved. Nothing had occurred for a long time that so hurt him. He loved honesty and truth; but how opposite to both had been the conduct of his boy!

"Go up to your chamber, and stay there until I see you or send for you," he said; and Arthur retired in shame from the presence of his parents, and the brother he had so meanly attempted to injure. Of course he felt very unhappy. How could he feel otherwise? The rebuking words of his father fell like heavy blows upon his heart, and the pain they occasioned was for a long time severely felt.

What punishment the parents thought it right to inflict upon Arthur we do not know; but, no doubt, he was punished in some way, as he deserved. And besides this, he had the still severer punishment which always follows that meanest fault of which any one can be guilty —that of accusing another and innocent person of what we have ourselves done.

Bad as this fault is, it is, alas! too common. But no manly, honest-minded, truthful boy will be betrayed into it. To the better impulses of our young readers who have been so wicked as to fall into this sin, either from sudden impulse or deliberate purpose, we would earnestly appeal, and beg of them to think more wisely and act more justly in the future. No cause is ever made better, but always worse, by a falsehood. Even where detection does not follow, suspicion is almost always created; for it is impossible for a boy to tell a lie without betraying it in the face or voice, and causing a doubt to pass through the minds of his parents, and set them to making inquiry into the truth or falsehood of what he has stated.

Truth—the open, bold, honest truth—is always the best, always the wisest, always the safest for every one, in any and all circumstances. Let no boy deviate from it, even though he have been guilty of a fault. Better—a thousand times better—is it to own to the wrong, and keep a clear conscience.

A Story about a Dog.

"TELL us a story, father, before we go to bed," said a little boy, who spoke for two brothers as well as for himself.

"What shall it be about?" asked Mr. Melville, their father.

"Oh, about a dog. I love to hear stories about dogs."

"Oh yes! let it be about a dog."

"Yes, papa, let it be about a dog," ran through the circle of children.

"Wouldn't you rather hear a story about the innocent lamb; the pure, snow-white lamb that sports in the green meadows?" said the father. "Dogs are evil animals."

"Oh no, father! dogs are not evil animals.

You don't call our Carlo an evil animal? He's a good, kind, generous dog. Didn't he save the life of Mr. Graham's little Harry, when he fell into the river? And doesn't he love us, and go with us everywhere? And didn't he jump on Mr. Parker's Nero and beat him, when he flew out at us as we were passing, and was going to bite us? I am sure Carlo is a good dog. He watches our house at night, and keeps all the robbers away."

"Carlo is one of the better class of dogs," said Mr. Melville. "Many of these animals have generous qualities, and can be taught by man to perform many good acts; but I hardly think the dog can be called a good animal, like the noble horse or the useful cow and sheep. These serve man in a great variety of ways, and do not, even in their wild state, prey upon other animals, or attack and injure man as the dog will. The only use of the dog is for a protection against evil; and he is able to do this from something in him that is cruel and destructive. But I own that in some dogs there are to be found many noble and generous qualities; but these they derive from long association with man, and from being employed by him from one generation to another in doing useful things. The dogs of St. Bernard, of which you have so often read, are noble specimens of this improved race. So are the Newfoundland dogs. But still they are not good and innocent,—like sheep, for instance, or cows, or like the gentle dove. Those are truly innocent animals, and correspond in nature to certain good affections in our minds."

But the children still thought that Carlo must be a good animal, and insisted that it was so, and upon having a story about a dog instead of a lamb.

"Very well," said Mr. Melville: "I will tell you a story about a dog, and a very interesting one it is too. I heard it or read about it somewhere recently, but I cannot now tell where."

"Tell it, father, do tell it," urged the children.

Mr. Melville then told the following story:—

"There was a boy,—we will call his name Thomas,—whose father bought him a fine horse, upon which he used to ride out almost every day, accompanied by a large Newfoundland dog named Bruno. One day Thomas had his horse brought out for a ride, and after he had mounted the animal, he whistled for Bruno, who was lying on a mat in front of the house. But Bruno only wagged his tail. He did not even lift his head from between his fore paws, although his dark bright eyes were fixed upon his young master. 'Come, Bruno, come!' called Thomas. But the dog only wagged his tail more quickly. 'You are a lazy fellow, Bruno,' said Thomas, in a half-chiding, disappointed tone. 'I shan't half enjoy my ride unless you come.' And he whistled loud for Bruno, as he gave his horse the rein and trotted off. Although he looked back and called for Bruno many times, as he rode away, the dog evinced no disposition to follow him.

"It was near sunset, and the father and mother of Thomas were sitting in front of their door, enjoying the cool refreshing air. Bruno still lay upon the mat, and seemed to be sleeping.

"'I wonder why that dog didn't go with Thomas?' said the father, looking at Bruno.

"'He's lazy to-day,' replied the mother.

'Thomas called him, and tried his best to get him off with him, as usual, but Bruno never stirred.'

"On hearing his name, the dog rose up, and came and rubbed himself against his master, who patted him kindly upon the head. While standing thus by his master's side, Bruno all at once pricked up his ears and rose, and seemed all attention. Almost at the same instant the father of Thomas heard the distant clattering of a horse's hoofs, which drew nearer every moment. He arose quickly; as he did so, Bruno gave a short, uneasy bark, and went a few steps towards the road, holding his head very high, and looking first in one direction and then in another. This suspense did not continue long. In less than a minute from the time the first distant sound was heard, they saw the horse of Thomas come dashing down the road at a fearful speed, with his little rider clinging to his neck. The house stood nearly a hundred yards from the road, and the horse approaching at such a rapid rate, that, although the father sprang forward to catch him, if possible, at the moment of passing, yet he was instantly conscious that before he could possibly reach the road the frightened animal would be beyond his reach. Just as his mind felt this painful certainty, Bruno went past him like an arrow, cleared the fence at a bound, and at the moment the horse was passing the gate caught him by the bridle. To this he held on, checking the animal's speed so much that his master found it easy to come up with and stop him."

"Oh, what a noble dog!" cried the children. "How Thomas must have loved him!"

"But how," said one, "did Bruno know that the horse was going to run away?"

"He did not know it," said Mr. Melville.

"Then why didn't he go with Thomas? He must have known it, father."

"Oh no; that doesn't follow, my son, at all. But the Lord, in his omnipotence and providence, knew what would take place, and provided just the means that were needed to save Thomas from being killed."

"Then he made Bruno stay at home that he might be ready to save his young master's life?" said one of the children.

"The Lord's protecting Spirit is everywhere,"

replied Mr. Melville, "and governs in all circumstances by which we are preserved from
harm. Without doubt, it was an influence
from Heaven that produced in the dog an in-
disposition to go with Thomas."

"How good the Lord is!" said the child who
had last spoken, in a thoughtful tone.

"Yes, my dear," returned Mr. Melville;
"the Lord is good to all, and kind even to the
unthankful. He maketh his sun to shine upon
the evil and the good, and sendeth his rain upon
the just and the unjust."

The Discontented Shepherd.

N a quiet valley there once dwelt a shepherd, who led a peaceful, happy life. He had large flocks, from whose fleecy backs the wool was regularly shorn, and sold to the merchants; and the merchants paid him money, with which he bought all things needful for health and bodily comfort.

One day the shepherd drove his flocks to the sea-side, and as he looked abroad upon the great expanse of water, and saw the ships moving over its surface, he felt, for the first time, discontented with his lot. A desire to see the world took possession of his mind.

"I will no longer shut myself up in this

narrow valley," he said. "I will become a
merchant. I will pass over the wide sea, and
go among the people of many lands."

So the shepherd sold his flocks, and with
the money bought merchandise, which he placed
in a ship, and started for a distant country.
During the first day after leaving the land, he
could do little else but admire the wonderful
ocean upon whose surface he was sailing, and
think how happy he was at having escaped the
dull life of a shepherd in an unknown vale.
But on the second day after leaving the land,
the motion of the ship made him very sick.
He could no longer enjoy the great expanse of
ocean and sky spread out above and around
him, but had to remain in the cabin, unable
even to lift his head from his pillow. As he
lay sick in the dark, narrow cabin, filled with
polluted air, he thought of the green shady
places, cool refreshing streams, and pure air of
his native valley, and, for the first time, he
repented of what he had done.

It was more than a week before the shepherd could go upon deck, and feel pleasure in
the sky and ocean as he had done at first.

At last the vessel arrived at its destined place : the shepherd landed his goods and offered them for sale. He soon found a merchant willing to buy them. The price was agreed upon, the merchandise delivered, and the money demanded. But it happened, as it almost always happens when men get dissatisfied with the business or calling with which they are perfectly familiar, and enter into one they know nothing about, the shepherd fell into dishonest hands. The merchant refused to pay him his money.

In order to get this wrong redressed, the shepherd called upon a magistrate of the country, who promised to see that justice was done to him. But the merchant knew the magistrate to be as unfitted for his calling as he was for his, and so he offered him a bribe, which the wicked magistrate accepted. In vain did the shepherd seek for justice at his hands ; no justice could he get. His importunities at last became so great, that the magistrate threatened to have him put into prison if he troubled him any more.

In his own peaceful valley there was no

wrong and oppression like this. The merchants who came for his fleece were good and true men, and paid the prices agreed upon. The ignorant shepherd had not dreamed that there were such wicked men in the world as this merchant and this magistrate, into whose hands he had fallen.

In a strange land, among strange people, thousands of miles away from his home, and all his money and property gone, the poor shepherd was about giving up in despair. But he bethought him that he would go to the king of the country, and ask justice at his hands.

The king, when he heard the shepherd's story, was very angry at the wrong that had been done in his kingdom. He sent immediately, and had the magistrate and the merchant brought before him and confronted with their accuser. On seeing the shepherd, their hearts became filled with alarm, and their faces betrayed what was in their hearts. When accused they could answer nothing. So the king caused the merchant to pay the shepherd for his goods; and besides, imposed upon him a heavy fine.   From the magistrate he took away his office, and had him cast into prison.

As soon as the shepherd had received his money, he returned in the first ship that sailed for his native country, and buying more flocks, was ever after contented to follow them in the peaceful valley where no wrong, oppression, or dishonesty had yet come.

The Shilling.

GEORGE HANSON'S uncle had given him a shilling; and George, like most boys, felt very anxious to spend it. But, among his many wants, he found it a hard matter to decide upon which to gratify. If it had been a half-crown instead of a shilling, the difficulty would have been lessened, for then George could have supplied at least half a dozen wants. But it was only a shilling.

He stood at the window, looking out upon the passengers who were going quickly by, the frosty air of December giving lightness to many a step that, in a milder day, would have been less hurriedly taken. While standing

here, his mind half made up to gratify his love
of cakes and oranges by a whole shilling's
worth, a man went by with some pretty little
glass toys in a box, which he held up to the
window, and asked if he did not want to buy
some.

George beckoned to the man to stop, and
then ran to the front door. The man was a
glass-blower, and had manufactured some handsome birds, and sheep, and deer, from white
glass, which looked, certainly, curious and
beautiful.

" How much is this ? " asked George, pointing to a bird of paradise.

" Eighteen-pence."

" But I've only got a shilling," returned
George.

" Well, here's a robin redbreast for a shilling ; and here's a deer, and a sheep. All
these on this side are a shilling."

But George liked the bird of paradise best
of all, and couldn't think of taking anything
else.

While the man stood trying to persuade him
to buy one of the birds that were sold for a

shilling, George looked up and saw going by a poor old man, who was bent with age. He led a little girl by the hand, who appeared to shrink in the cold. The old man looked sick and feeble, and very poor.

"They shall have my shilling!" exclaimed George, speaking from a sudden impulse; and he stepped forward, and placing the coin in the old man's hand, said, as he did so,—

"I was just going to spend this for a little glass toy that would be broken in a day. But I want it put to a better use. Take it, and buy something for your little girl."

The poor old man stopped, and said, with a look of surprise and pleasure as he received the coin,—

"Thank you, my young master! This will give my little Alice a nice bowl of bread and milk for her supper and breakfast. She will think of you with a grateful heart while she eats them."

"Well done, my good boy!" said the glass-blower, as the old man went on his way. "That poor little girl's bread and milk will taste sweet to her to-night. And as a reward for your generous self-denial, here is the bird of paradise that has pleased you so much : take it."

But George drew back, and said he hardly thought that would be right.

"Why not, I wonder?" returned the man. "Am I to be outdone in generosity by a boy? Take it, and whenever you look upon it let it teach you this lesson—that it is more blessed to give than to receive; for I am sure the thought of the good done to the old man and the little girl will be more pleasant to you than the thought of possessing this pretty toy."

And so it was. The toy pleased for a short time only, but the thought of the little girl who had been made happy by his shilling never passed through his mind without giving him pleasure.

The Wounded Bird.

"FATHER," said Henry Thompson, a boy just eleven years old, "won't you buy me a gun?"

"A gun! Oh no; I can't buy you a gun," Mr. Thompson replied in a decided voice.

Henry turned away disappointed, and went out of his father's warehouse, into which he had come specially to ask for a gun. He was not pleased at the refusal he had met with, and felt much inclined, as are too many children, to indulge hard thoughts against his kind father for not gratifying his wish. As he walked along, he met Alfred Lyon, a lad about his own age, whose father had

given him a gun, and who then had it on his
shoulder.

"Come, Henry," said Alfred, "I'm going out
a-shooting. Won't you go with me?"

Henry at once said "Yes." It was a holiday, and his mother had told him that he
might go out and spend the morning as he
liked, only that he must not go into danger,
nor harm anything. So he did not hesitate to
go with Alfred. He had seen the little boy
the day before, and then learned that he had
received from his father the present of a gun,
and this was what had made him desire to
have one also.

The two little boys then took their way to
the woods. It was a bright day in early sum-
mer. The trees were all covered with tender
foliage, the fields bright and green, and the
singing birds made the air thrill with delicious
melody. To mar this scene of innocence, beauty,
and peace, came these two thoughtless boys.
They saw the woods mantled in their dark,
rich drapery, that moved gracefully in the light
breeze; but all their majestic beauty was lost
to their eyes. They thought only whether the

thick, green masses of leaves contained a robin or harmless red-bird, as a victim to their murderous gun. The green fields, too, were pleasant to their eyes only so far as they might conceal, in their blossoming hedgerows, a victim wren or sparrow. And the sweet trilling of the lovely songsters, as it floated from wood and field, though it gladdened their ears, affected them not with a pure and innocent pleasure. I grieve to make such a record of these two lads, but it is, alas! too true. Both together, were they to labour over their task from this hour of their boyhood until threescore and ten years had been numbered to them, could not make even a little yellow bird,—nay, not so much as a feather like one shed from its downy wing; and yet they were eager to destroy the lovely creature made by God's own hand, and all from an idle love of sport.

Well, Alfred and Henry soon arrived at the woods.

"Hark!" said Alfred, "there is a robin singing in that maple! Be still, and I will shoot him."

Henry stood very still, while Alfred moved

stealthily along, with his gun in his hand, until he stood nearly under the maple-tree. The robin, all unconscious of danger, was singing his song of gladness—a tribute of praise to Him who had fashioned him curiously, and with inconceivable wisdom and skill—when the boy raised his gun, took a deadly aim, and fired. The breast of the robin was still heaving, and his throat trembling with the song, when the swift-winged shot entered his side, and pierced his little heart. He fell at the feet of his murderer. One would have thought, that when Alfred and Henry saw the bleeding bird, lying dead on the ground, their hearts would have been filled with sorrow. But not so. A shout of joy followed this cruel exploit. The bird was picked up, and a string tied about its neck, and borne along with them, as the triumphant evidence of Alfred's skill with his weapon.

Next an oriole was discovered, flying from a bush near them, and alighting upon the branch of a tree, high up in the air.

"Now, let me shoot," said Henry; and Alfred suffered his companion to take the gun.

He proved to be not quite so good a marksman as Alfred.   But he struck the oriole, and wounded him.   The bird fluttered to another tree, upon a limb of which he alighted.   Here he clung, with his tiny feet, until these cruel boys had again loaded their gun.   Then Henry took a truer aim, and brought him to the ground.   But he was not dead.   Henry seized the trembling creature, that tried in vain to escape, and held him fast in his hands.

"Wring off his neck," said Alfred; "that's the way."

"No, no," returned Henry; "I'll take him home just as he is: perhaps he'll get well, and then I'll put him in a cage, and keep him."

And so Henry kept the bird, that must have been suffering great pain, carefully in his hand, while Alfred loaded his gun once more.   But we will not follow these boys further in their cruel employment, which was continued for several hours, when they grew tired, and returned home.   It was past the dinner hour when Henry got back, with four birds for his share of the morning's sport.   One of these was the oriole, still alive.   Another was a sparrow, another a robin, and the fourth a blue-bird. These last three were all dead.

"Just see, mother, what I've got; and I killed them all myself," cried Henry, as he came in and displayed his birds. "Won't you ask father to buy me a gun? Alfred Lyon has got one, and I think I ought to have one too. I asked father to-day to buy me one, but he said *No.* Won't you ask him to buy me a gun, mother? for I can shoot; I shot all these with Alfred's gun, myself."

Henry's mother listened to her son with surprise and pain. "Poor bird!" said she, taking from Henry the wounded oriole, and handling it with great tenderness. "Can it be possible that my son has done this?——that his hand has committed so cruel a deed?" and the tears dimmed her eyes.

The words, tone, and manner of his mother touched the heart of Henry in an instant. New thoughts were awakened, and with these thoughts came new feelings. His mind had a glimpse of the truth, that it was wrong to sport with the life of any creature.

"Can you make a pretty bird like this?" his

mother asked, pointing to the drooping bird in her hand.　Her son was silent.

"Then why seek, wantonly, to take its life?" she continued.　"Were you envious of its happiness?　Like an evil spirit, did a sight of innocent delights inflame you with a desire to destroy it?　Can you restore health to its wounded body?　No!　Can you ever assuage its present agonies?　No—you cannot.　Cruel boy! what could you have been dreaming about?　Think, how terrible it would be, if there were a race of beings stronger than we are, who, with the power, had the will to destroy us for mere sport.　Some day I might be walking out, and become the victim of one of these, and then my children would have no mother.　Perhaps Henry might leave me, and while on his way to school might be shot at, as he shot at the birds, and be killed like this pretty blue-bird, or fatally wounded like this oriole.　Would you think such sport innocent?　I think not.　Poor bird!　See how it trembles!　See how it flutters its wings in pain!　See how it gasps!　Now it has fallen over upon its side——and now it is dead!　Alas, that my son should have done this cruel deed—that my son should have caused all this pain!"

The words of Henry's mother touched him deeply. They caused him to see how cruel he had indeed been. They made him conscious that it was most wicked to hurt or kill any one of God's creatures in mere sport. So moved was he, that he could not refrain from bursting into tears and sobbing bitterly.

"O mother!" he said, after he had gained some little command over his feelings, "I never thought how wicked and cruel it was to take pleasure in hunting the pretty birds. I don't want a gun. I wouldn't have a gun now, if father would buy me the handsomest one in town."

Henry's mother was glad to hear him say this, for it showed that he felt all she wished him to feel—sorrow at having indulged in a cruel sport. It showed, also, that he had determined in his own mind, from seeing how wicked it was, never to do so again. From this determination Henry never swerved. He was never known afterwards to hurt any animal in sport. And more than this, by talk-

ing to his little friend Alfred, he caused him to
see how wrong it was to shoot the birds; and
Alfred gave his gun back to his father, who
sold it for him, and with the money bought
him a number of good and useful books.

The Holiday.

"HOW are you going to spend your holiday?" asked Edgar Williams of Charles Manly.

"I don't know; how are you going to spend yours?"

"I'm going a-fishing; won't you go with me?"

"No, I think not," replied Manly.

"Why? It will be fine sport."

But Manly shook his head, and replied,—

"I don't think it such fine sport to hunt the little fishes. I'm sure I shouldn't like a sharp hook in my mouth. Ugh! To think of being lifted up by a hook fastened in your tongue, or in the roof of your mouth!"

"You're very tender-hearted all at once," replied Edgar Williams. "I've seen you fishing, many a time."

"No doubt of it. But I hardly think I shall go again. Father says it is cruel sport; and so it is. Suppose you don't go, Edgar."

"Oh yes, but I will. It's delightful. I'm fond of it above everything."

"I'll tell you what I should like to do, if you would go with me," said Charles Manly.

"Well?"

"I should like to go out into the woods and fields, to look for specimens for my cabinet."

"A fig for specimens!" returned Williams. "No, indeed! I'm going a-fishing."

The two lads had each some money given to him by his parents to spend. With his money, Edgar Williams bought a fishing-line, a rod, and some bait; and taking his dinner in a basket, started off alone to spend his day in fishing from the river-bank. During the morning the fish would not bite. Hour after hour he threw his line in vain. He did not get so much as a nibble. About midday, tired and disappointed, Edgar threw his

rod upon the grass, and now beginning to feel
hungry, he opened his lunch-basket and took
therefrom his dinner, the eating of which he
enjoyed much more than he had enjoyed his
fishing. After this, he lay down under the
shade of a tree and slept for an hour. When
he awoke, he felt dull and heavy, and wished
himself at home. But he had caught nothing,
and did not want to go back with so poor an
account of his doings. So he took up his rod
and line, and again sought to take the life, for
mere sport, of some fish, tempted, in the hope
of obtaining food, to seize upon the murderous
hook. But his red cork lay, as before, im-
movable upon the smooth surface of the river
for a very long time. At last it suddenly dis-
appeared, and Edgar gave his line a quick jerk,
which brought up a bright little sunfish, that
had hoped to get a good dinner, but was, alas!
sadly disappointed. It was not more than
three inches long, and beautiful to look upon as
a fish could be, so thin, so delicately made,
and so purely golden in its hue. Edgar caught
the fluttering little creature in his hand, and
tore the cruel hook from its bleeding mouth,

Just at that moment he thought of what Charles Manly had said, about having a sharp hook in his tongue or tearing into the roof of his mouth, and for the first time in his life he felt pity for a fish. The quivering little animal was still in his hand, and he held it up and looked at its torn mouth, with the blood oozing therefrom, and sorrow for the pain he had occasioned touched his heart.

"It is cruel sport, as Charles said, sure enough," he murmured to himself. "This little fish never did me any harm. And even if I were in want of food, which I am not, it is too small to eat. So I have no excuse for doing it this sad injury. Go, little fish!" he added, throwing it back again into the river. "I will not rob you of life, though I have seriously injured you."

But the fish, instead of diving down out of sight into the deep water, turned upon its side and swam about unevenly upon the surface of the water. Edgar felt grieved when he saw this.

"Poor little sunfish," he said; "I hope you will not die."

Just then he observed a sudden rippling motion of the water, a short distance from where the sunfish was swimming about, and in an instant afterwards the little sufferer was seized by some larger fish and devoured.

"I'll never fish again for sport!" said Edgar, throwing his rod and line into the water, and turning sadly away from the river-side.

It was nearly night when he arrived at home, tired and altogether dissatisfied with himself. More than an hour elapsed after he went to bed before he could close his eyes in sleep. The image of that beautiful little sunfish, with its torn and bleeding mouth, was too vividly present to his mind. During the night, he dreamed that he fell into the river, and was seized by some monster, as he had seen the sunfish seized. He awoke in terror, with the perspiration starting from every pore, and it was a long time before sleep visited his eyes again.

Sweeter far, and more peaceful, were the dreams of Charles Manly, who had gone with his sister to the museum, and spent his holiday there, examining the many curious and wonderful things in art and nature that it contained. His enjoyment had been innocent, and it had left his mind tranquil and peaceful.

Rober and his Little Master.

"COME, Rover!" said Harry, as he passed a fine old Newfoundland dog that lay on a mat at the door; "come, Rover! I am going down to the river to sail my boat, and I want you to go with me."

Rover opened his large eyes, and looked lazily at his little master.

"Come, Rover!—Rover!"

But the dog didn't care to move, and so Harry went off to the river-side alone. He had not been gone a great while, before a thought of her boy came suddenly into the mother's mind. Remembering that he had a little vessel, and that the river was near, it occurred to her that he might have gone there.

Instantly her heart began to throb with alarm.

"Is Harry with you?" she called up to Harry's father, who was in his study. But Harry's father said he was not there.

"I'm afraid he's gone to the river with his boat," said the mother.

"To the river!" And Mr. Lee dropped his pen, and came quickly down. Taking up his hat, he went hurriedly from the house. Rover was still lying upon the mat, with his head upon his paws and his eyes shut.

"Rover!" said his master, in a quick, excited voice, "where is Harry? Has he gone to the river? Away and see! quick!"

The dog must have understood every word, for he sprang eagerly to his feet, and rushed toward the river. Mr. Lee followed as fast as he could run. When he reached the river-bank, he saw his little boy in the water, with Rover dragging him towards the shore. He was just in time to receive the half-drowned child in his arms, and carry him home to his mother.

Harry, who remained insensible, was placed

in a warm bed. He soon, however, revived,
and in an hour or two was running about again.
But after this, Rover would never leave the
side of his little master, when he wandered
beyond the garden gate. Wherever you found
Harry, there Rover was sure to be—sometimes
walking by his side, and sometimes lying on
the grass, with his big eyes watching every
movement.

Once Harry found his little vessel, which
had been hidden away since he went with it
to the river, and, without his mother seeing
him, he started again for the water. Rover,
as usual, was with him. On his way to the
river he saw some flowers, and, in order to
gather them, put his boat down upon the grass.
Instantly Rover picked it up in his mouth, and
walked back towards the house with it. After
going a little way, he stopped, looked round,
and waited until Harry had got his hand full
of flowers. The child then saw that Rover
had his boat, and tried to get it from him ; but
Rover played round him, always keeping out
of his reach, and retreating towards the house,
until he got back within the gate. Then he

bounded into the house, and laid the boat at the feet of Harry's mother.

Harry was a little angry with the good old dog, at first; but when his mother explained to him what Rover meant, he hugged him round the neck, and said he would never go down to the river any more.

Harry is a man now, and Rover has long since been dead; but he often thinks of the dear old dog that saved him from drowning when he was a child; and it gives him great pleasure to remember that he never beat Rover, as some boys beat their dogs, when they are angry, and was never unkind to him. Had it been otherwise, the thought would have given him great pain.

James and Henry;

OR, "TWO WRONGS NEVER MAKE A RIGHT."

——◆——

MOTHER, who loved her children very much, sat reading a good book one day, while her two little boys were playing in the next room. All at once loud cries and angry words fell upon her ears, and gave her great pain. She rose up quickly, and went in to the children, and there she saw a sad sight indeed. James, her eldest boy, whose eighth birthday had just been passed, was standing over his younger brother, Henry, with his hand raised, and his face red with anger; and Henry had doubled his little fist, and was ready to strike again.

" James ! Henry ! " cried their mother, as soon as her eyes fell upon them.

" Mother ! mother ! Henry knocked over my house, and he did it on purpose," said the eldest boy, a blush of shame covering his face, and hiding the red anger that was on it an instant before.

" No, mother, I didn't do it on purpose," spoke up little Henry. " It was an accident ; and he struck me."

"And then what did you do ?" asked the mother, taking the little boy by the hand, and looking him in the face.

Henry held down his head, and replied, " I struck him again."

" Oh, how wrong that was ! "

" But I didn't mean to knock over his house."

" How was it, James ? " the mother asked, appealing to the eldest boy.

" He did knock over my house."

" But, do you believe it was done on purpose ? "

" He kept pushing his foot against it all the while, and I told him not to do it," said James.

" Why, Henry ? "

Henry again hung down his head, and was silent.

"And so you did it on purpose, Henry?"

"Oh no, no, mother, I didn't do it on purpose," cried Henry, bursting into tears and burying his face in his mother's lap. "It was an accident. I did put my foot against the house, *just to plague him;* but I didn't mean to push it over. *Something made my foot go hard against it.* But I am sorry."

And Henry sobbed aloud.

"Henry is sorry for what he has done, James; he did not do it on purpose. But you were angry and struck him on purpose. Are you not sorry?"

"But he was trying to plague me; and he is always trying to plague me."

"That was wrong, James. But, you know that I have often said to you—*two wrongs never make a right.* Do you feel any happier now, because you struck your brother?"

James was silent.

"Tell me, my son, do you think you are happier for what you have done?"

The little boy said, "No."

"But you feel very unhappy?"

"Yes, mother."

"That is a sign that you have done wrong. When we do right it makes us happy. Are you not always sorry after you have done wrong?"

"Yes, mother."

"You are sorry that you struck Henry?"

"Yes, ma'am."

"And Henry is sorry for having tried to plague you; ain't you, Henry?"

"Yes, ma'am."

"Then give James your hand, my son. He is sorry for having struck you."

The little boys took hold of each other's hands, and looked into each other's faces. But tears were in both their eyes, and on their cheeks.

"Now kiss each other with the kiss of forgiveness."

The children put their arms round each other's necks, and kissed each other with a warm kiss of love and forgiveness.

"Now bring me that little book lying on the table, James," said the mother.

James brought the book, and the mother opened it, and read :—

> " ' Whatever brawls disturb the street,
> There should be peace at home ;
> Where sisters dwell, and brothers meet,
> Quarrels should never come.

> " ' Birds in their little nests agree,
> And 'tis a shameful sight,
> When children of one family
> Fall out, and chide, and fight.

> " ' Hard names at first, and angry words,
> Which are but noisy breath,
> May come to clubs and naked swords,
> To murder and to death.'

"Think of that, my dear children! 'To murder and to death!' If you quarrel with each other now, instead of growing up and loving each other, you may grow up to hate each other. I remember two brothers that were once no older than you are. They were always quarrelling with each other, and they kept on quarrelling as they grew up. One day, after they had become men, they got into a dispute about something, when one of them struck the other a dreadful blow with a stick and killed him. Was not that a terrible thing? And who knows but that you, if you keep on quarrelling as you do now, may grow up to hate one another."

"Henry, do you know why it is that you so often try to tease your brother James?"

"Yes, ma'am."

"Why is it, my son?"

"I let evil spirits come into me, and do what they wish me to do."

"Yes, that is the reason. But can't you keep them out."

"Yes, ma'am, if I try."

"Do you like to have evil spirits in you, instead of good angels."

"Oh no. I love the good angels, and I hate the wicked spirits that make me do wrong."

"How can you keep the wicked spirits out?"

"By not doing the wrong things they want me to do, and then the good angels will drive them all away."

"I hope, my dear children, as you know so well what is right, that you will never again let wicked spirits from hell have anything to do with you. When they again tempt you to plague your brother, Henry, you must not do it, and then they will go away; and you, James,

if Henry should again be so weak and foolish
as to let the evil spirits come into him, must
not let them come into you at the same time.
If, instead of letting them tempt you to
strike him, you permit the good angels to
govern you, you will speak kindly to him, and
say, 'Don't, brother, please.' I am sure he
will do so no longer. By doing this, you will
help him to cast out the evil spirits who are
seeking to destroy him."

"How destroy him, mother?"

"All evil spirits seek to destroy children by
making them wicked like themselves, so that
they may be cast into hell. They hate
children so much, that, if they were not re-
strained by the Lord, they would do them all
manner of harm—would utterly destroy them;
for they burn with hatred towards little children."

"But the Lord won't let them hurt us."

"Not if we will keep them out of our hearts.
But if we let them come in, he cannot save us.
And, whenever you are angry with each other,
they come into your little hearts. Oh! my
dear children, keep out these dreadful enemies,
or they will utterly destroy you."

The children burst into tears, kissed each other and their mother again and again, and promised that they would try and never speak or act unkindly to one another as long as they lived. We hope they will not; and that all our little readers will try, like them, to keep evil spirits far away, that good angels may be round about them and dwell in their young hearts.

The Use of Flowers.

———◆———

UST one moment longer, cousin Mary ; I want to put this flower in your hair. Now doesn't it look sweet, sister Aggy ? "

"Oh yes! very sweet. And here is the dearest little bud I ever saw. I took it from the sweet-brier bush in the lane. Put that, too, in cousin Mary's hair."

Little Florence, seeing what was going on, was soon also at work upon Mary's hair, which, in a little while, was covered with buds and blossoms.

"Now she is our May Queen," said the chil-dren, as they hung fondly around their cousin, who had come into the country to enjoy a few weeks of rural quiet, in the season of fruits and flowers.

"And our May Queen must sing us a song," said Agnes, who was sitting at the feet of her cousin. "Sing us something about flowers."

"Oh yes!" spoke up Grace; "sing us that beautiful piece by Mrs. Howitt, about the use of flowers. You sang it for us, you remember, the last time you were here."

Cousin Mary sang as desired. After she had concluded, she said,—

"Flowers, according to these beautiful verses, are only useful as objects to delight our senses. They are only beautiful forms in nature—their highest use, their beauty and fragrance."

"I think that is what Mrs. Howitt means," replied Grace. "So I have always understood her. And I cannot see any other use that flowers have. Do you know of any other use, cousin?"

"Oh yes. Flowers have a more important use than merely giving delight to the senses. Without them, plants could not produce fruit and seed. You notice that the flower always comes before the fruit?"

"Oh yes. But why is a flower needed? Why does not the fruit push itself directly out from the stem of a plant?" asked Agnes.

"Flowers are the most exquisitely delicate in their texture of all forms in the vegetable kingdom. Look at the petals of this one. Could anything be softer or finer? The leaf, the bark, and the wood of the plant are all coarse, in comparison to the flower. Now, as nothing is made in vain, there must be some reason for this. The leaves and bark, as well as wood, of plants, all have vessels through which sap flows, and this sap nourishes, sustains, and builds up the plant, as our blood does our bodies. But the whole effort of the plant is to reproduce itself; and to this end it forms seed, which, when cast into the ground, takes root, springs up, and makes a new plant. To form this seed requires the purest juices of the plant, and these are obtained by means of the flowers, through the exquisitely fine vessels of which these juices are filtered, or strained, and thus separated from all that is gross and impure."

"I never thought of that before," said

Agnes. "Flowers, then, are useful as well as beautiful."

"Nothing is made for mere beauty. All things in nature regard use as an end. To flowers are assigned a high and important use, and exquisite beauty of form and colour is at the same time given to them ; and with these our senses are delighted. They are, in more respects than one, good gifts from our heavenly Father."

"Oh! how I do love the flowers," said Agnes ; "and now, when I look upon them, and think of their use as well as their beauty, I shall love them still more. Are they so very beautiful because their use is such an important one, cousin Mary ? "

"Yes, dear ; I believe this is so. In the seeds of plants there is an image of the infinity of our great Creator ; for in seeds resides a power, or an effort, to reproduce the plants, that lie concealed as gems within them, to infinity. We might naturally enough suppose that flowers, whose use it is to refine and prepare the juices of plants, so as to free them from all grosser matters, and make them fit for the important

office of developing and maturing seeds, would
be exceedingly delicate in their structure, and,
as a natural consequence, beautiful to look upon.
And we will believe, therefore, that their peculiar beauty depends upon their peculiar use."

Books of Precept and Example.

Lives of Labour; or, Incidents in the Career of Eminent Naturalists and Celebrated Travellers. By C. L. BRIGHTWELL. With Six Coloured Plates. Post 8vo, cloth. Price 3s. 6d.

Living in Earnest. Lessons and Incidents from the Lives of the Great and Good. By JOSEPH JOHNSON. Post 8vo, cloth. Price 2s. 6d.

Doing Good; or, The Christian in Walks of Usefulness. Illustrated by Examples. By the Rev. R. STEEL, D.D. Post 8vo, cloth extra. Price 3s. 6d.

Willing Hearts and Ready Hands; or, The Labours and Triumphs of Earnest Women. By JOSEPH JOHNSON. Post 8vo, cloth extra. Price 3s. 6d.

Frank Oldfield; or, Lost and Found. By the Rev. T. P. WILSON, M.A. With Five Engravings. Post 8vo, cloth. Price 3s. 6d.

Tim's Troubles; or, Tried and True. By M. A. PAUL. With Five Engravings. Post 8vo, cloth. Price 3s. 6d.

The Threshold of Life. A Book of Illustrations and Lessons for the Encouragement and Counsel of Youth. By W. H. DAVENPORT ADAMS. With Six Engravings. Post 8vo, cloth. Price 2s. 6d.

Learn to Labour and to Wait; or, The Story of the Townshends and their Neighbours. By MARION E. WEIR. With Six Engravings. Post 8vo, cloth. Price 2s. 6d.

Seed-Time and Harvest; or, Sow Well and Reap Well. A Book for the Young. By the late Rev. W. K. TWEEDIE, D.D. With Coloured Frontispiece and Vignette, and Six Tinted Plates. Post 8vo, cloth. Price 2s. 6d.

Kind Words Awaken Kind Echoes. With Coloured Frontispiece and Vignette, and Six Tinted Plates. Post 8vo, cloth, gilt edges. Price 3s.

Tales with Useful Morals.

Stepping Heavenward. A Tale of Home Life. By the Author of "The Flower of the Family." Post 8vo, cloth. Price 2s. 6d.

By the same Author.

Ever Heavenward; or, A Mother's Influence. Post 8vo, cloth. Price 2s. 6d.

The Flower of the Family. A Tale of Domestic Life. Post 8vo, cloth. Price 2s. 6d.

Herman; or, The Little Preacher: Little Threads: and, The Story Lizzie Told. With Four Illustrations printed in Colours. Post 8vo, cloth extra. Price 2s. 6d.

Waiting and Winning; or, Bread Cast upon the Waters and Found After Many Days. With Four Illustrations printed in Colours. Post 8vo, cloth extra. Price 2s. 6d.

Willing to be Useful; or, Principle and Duty Illustrated in the Story of Edith Allison. With Seven Tinted Plates. Post 8vo, cloth. Price 2s.

The Grey House on the Hill; or, "Buy the Truth and Sell it Not." A Tale for the Young. By the Hon. Mrs. GREENE. Post 8vo, cloth. Price 2s. 6d.

The King's Highway; or, Illustrations of the Commandments. By the Rev. RICHARD NEWTON, D.D. With numerous Engravings. Post 8vo, cloth. Price 2s.

Stories of the Lives of Noble Women. By W. H. DAVENPORT ADAMS. Post 8vo, cloth. Price 2s. 6d.

Watch—Work—Wait. A Story of the Battle of Life. By SARAH MYERS. Foolscap 8vo, cloth. Price 2s.

Praise and Principle; or, For What Shall I Live? A Tale. Illustrated. Post 8vo, cloth. Price 2s. 6d.

The Golden Rule; or, Do to Others as You would have Others do to You. Illustrated. Foolscap 8vo, cloth. Price 1s. 6d.

Tales for the Home Circle.

Anna Lee: Maiden, Wife, Mother. By T. S. ARTHUR. Post 8vo, cloth. Price 2s.

Sow Well and Reap Well. By T. S. Arthur. Illustrated. Post 8vo. Price 2s.

True Riches; or, Wealth Without Wings. By T. S. ARTHUR. Illustrated. Post 8vo. Price 2s.

Little Snowdrop and her Golden Casket. By the Author of "Little Hazel, the King's Messenger," &c. With Coloured Frontispiece and Vignette. Post 8vo, cloth. Price 2s. 6d.

Under the Old Oaks; or, Won by Love. By the Author of "Little Hazel, the King's Messenger," &c. With Coloured Frontispiece and Vignette. Post 8vo, cloth. Price 2s. 6d.

Little Hazel, the King's Messenger. By the Author of "Little Snowdrop and her Golden Casket," &c. With Coloured Frontispiece and Vignette. Post 8vo, cloth. Price 2s. 6d.

The Crown of Glory; or, "Faithful unto Death." A Scottish Story of Martyr Times. By the Author of "Little Hazel, the King's Messenger," &c. Post 8vo, cloth extra. Price 2s. 6d.

Lizzie Hepburn; or, Every Cloud has a Silver Lining. With Four Illustrations printed in Colours. Post 8vo, cloth. Price 2s. 6d.

Father's Coming Home. A Tale for the Young. By the Author of "Village Missionaries, &c. With Seven Illustrations. Post 8vo, cloth. Price 2s.

The Story of Little Robinson of Paris; or, The Triumphs of Industry. Translated from the French by LUCY LANDON. Illustrated. Cloth. Price 2s.

Illustrated Story-Books

FOR THE YOUNG.

BY THE AUTHOR OF "HOPE ON," ETC,

One Shilling and Sixpence each.   Royal 18mo.

The Fisherman's Children; or, The Sunbeam of Hardrick Cove.   With **Coloured** Frontispiece and Vignette, **and** Seventeen Engravings.

Susy's Flowers; or, "Blessed are the Merciful, for They shall obtain Mercy."   With Coloured Frontispiece and Vignette, and Twenty Engravings.

Brother Reginald's Golden Secret.   A Tale for the Young.   With Coloured Frontispiece and Vignette, **and** Twenty Engravings.

King Jack of Haylands.   A Tale of School Life. With Coloured Frontispiece **and Vignette, and** Eighteen Engravings.

One Shilling each.   Royal 18mo.

Little Aggie's Fresh Snowdrops, and What They did **in One** Day.   With **Coloured** Frontispiece and Vignette, **and** Thirty Engravings.

The Boy Artist. A Tale. With Coloured Frontispiece **and Vignette,** and numerous Engravings.

Hope On; or, The House that Jack Built.   With Coloured Frontispiece and Vignette, **and** Twenty-five Engravings.

Martha's Home, and how the Sunshine **came into it.** With Coloured Frontispiece **and** Vignette, **and** Thirty **Engravings.**

T. NELSON AND SONS, LONDON, EDINBURGH, AND NEW YORK.

Travel and Research
IN BIBLE LANDS.

The Land and the Book; or, Biblical Illustrations Drawn from the Manners and Customs, the Scenes and Scenery of the Holy Land. By the Rev. W. M. Thomson, D.D. Crown 8vo, 718 pages, with Twelve Coloured Illustrations and One Hundred and Twenty Woodcuts. Price 7s. 6d., cloth; morocco, 15s.

In the Holy Land. By the Rev. Andrew Thomson, D.D., Edinburgh, Author of "Great Missionaries." With Eighteen Engravings. Crown 8vo, cloth extra. Price 6s. 6d.

Bashan's Giant Cities and Syria's Holy Places. By Professor Porter, Author of "Murray's Hand-book to Syria and Palestine." With Eight Beautiful Engravings. Post 8vo, cloth extra. Price 7s. 6d.

IMPORTANT RELIGIOUS WORKS.

Systematic Theology. By Charles Hodge, D.D., Professor in the Theological Seminary, Princeton, New Jersey. Three vols. Royal 8vo. Price £2, 2s. Index vol., 3s. 6d. extra.

Outlines of Theology. By the Rev. A. A. Hodge, D.D., Princeton. Edited by the Rev. W. H. Goold, D.D., Edinburgh. Crown 8vo, cloth. Price 6s. 6d.

The Ministry of the Word. Being the "Yale College Lectures" for 1876. By the Rev. William M. Taylor, D.D., New York. Crown 8vo, cloth. Price 4s. 6d.

Commentary on the Confession of Faith. By A. A. Hodge, D.D. Edited by W. H. Goold, D.D. Post 8vo, cloth. Price 3s. 6d.

Darwinism, and its Relation to the Truths of Natural and Revealed Religion. By Charles Hodge, D.D., Princeton, Author of "Systematic Theology." Post 8vo, cloth. Price 3s. 6d.

WORKS

By the Author of "The Spanish Brothers."

Under the Southern Cross: **A Tale of the New** World. By the Author of "The Spanish Brothers." Crown 8vo, cloth. Price 6s. 6d.

The Spanish Brothers. A Tale of the Sixteenth Century. Crown 8vo, cloth extra. Price 6s. 6d.

No Cross No Crown; or, The Dark Year of Dundee. A Tale of the Scottish Reformation. With Seven Illustrations. Post 8vo. Price 3s. 6d.

INTERESTING TALES BY ANNIE LUCAS.

The City and the Castle. A Story of the Reformation in Switzerland. By ANNIE LUCAS, Author of "Léonie." Crown 8vo, cloth extra. Price 6s. 6d.

Leonie; or, Light Out of Darkness: and Within Iron Walls, a Tale of the Siege of Paris. Twin-Stories of the Franco-German War. By ANNIE LUCAS. Crown 8vo, cloth extra. Price 6s. 6d.

Pendower. A Story of Cornwall in the Reign of Henry the Eighth. By M. FILLEUL. Crown 8vo, cloth. Price 6s. 6d.

BY THE REV. J. C. RYLE.

The Christian Leaders of the Last Century; or, England a Hundred Years Ago. By the Rev. J. C. RYLE, B.A., Christ Church, Oxford. Crown 8vo, cloth. Price 7s. 6d.

BY THE LATE REV. WILLIAM ARNOT.

Laws from Heaven for Life on Earth. Crown 8vo, cloth. Price 7s. 6d.

The Parables of our Lord. Crown 8vo, cloth. Price 7s. 6d.

The Anchor of the Soul, and other Sermons. Crown 8vo, cloth. Price 5s.

The "Schönberg-Cotta" Series.

Crown 8vo. Cloth, 6s. 6d. each.

Chronicles of the Schönberg-Cotta Family.

The Victory of the Vanquished: A Story of the First Century.

Diary of Mrs. Kitty Trevylyan: A Story of the Times of Whitefield and the Wesleys.

The Draytons and the Davenants: A Story of the Civil Wars.

On Both Sides of the Sea: A Story of the Commonwealth and the Restoration.

Winifred Bertram, and the World she Lived in.

The Martyrs of Spain and the Liberators of Holland; or, The Story of the Sisters Dolores and Costanza Cazalla.

Sketches of Christian Life in England in the Olden Time.

Diary of Brother Bartholomew, with Other Tales and Sketches of Christian Life in Different Lands and Ages.

Wanderings Over Bible Lands and Seas. With Panorama of Jerusalem.

Poems by the Author of "Chronicles of the Schönberg-Cotta Family." CONTENTS:—The Women of the Gospels—The Three Wakings—Songs and Hymns—Memorial Verses. Gilt edges.

The Voice of Christian Life in Song; or, Hymns and Hymn-Writers of Many Lands and Ages.

T. NELSON AND SONS, LONDON, EDINBURGH, AND NEW YORK

Home Books
OF EXAMPLE AND ENCOURAGEMENT.

Home: A Book for the Family. By the late Rev. W. K. TWEEDIE, D.D. Post 8vo, cloth extra. Price 3s.

Schoolboy Heroes: The Story of Maurice Gray and Carl Adler. By the late Rev. J. W. ALEXANDER, D.D. With Coloured Frontispiece and Vignette, and Six Tinted Plates. Extra foolscap. Price 2s. 6d.

Success in Life: What it is, and how Attained. A Book for Young Men. With Coloured Frontispiece and Vignette, and Six Tinted Plates. Extra foolscap 8vo, cloth extra. Price 3s.

"Above Rubies;" or, Memorials of Christian Gentlewomen. By Miss C. L. BRIGHTWELL. Post 8vo, cloth extra, gilt edges. Price 3s. 6d.

The Early Choice. A Book for Daughters. By the late Rev. W. K. TWEEDIE, D.D. With Six Steel Plates. Post 8vo, gilt edges. Price 3s. 6d.

The Daughter at School. By the Rev. John TODD, D.D., Author of "The Student's Guide," &c. With Coloured Frontispiece and Vignette, and Six Tinted Plates. Post 8vo, cloth extra. Price 2s. 6d.

Youthful Diligence and Future Greatness. By the late Rev. W. K. TWEEDIE, D.D. With Coloured Frontispiece and Vignette, and Six Tinted Plates. Extra foolscap 8vo, cloth. Price 2s. 6d.

Memorials of Early Genius, and Remarkable Records of its Achievements. By the Author of "Success in Life." With Eight Tinted Plates. Post 8vo, cloth extra. Price 2s. 6d.

Self-Taught Men. A Series of Biographies. With Coloured Frontispiece and Vignette. Extra foolscap, cloth. Price 2s. 6d.